THROUGH GLACIER PARK

MARY ROBERTS RINEHART

FOREWORD BY RICK RINEHART

TWODOT®

GUILFORD, CONNECTICUT
HELENA, MONTANA

A · TWODOT® · BOOK

An imprint and registered trademark of Rowman & Littlefield

Distributed by NATIONAL BOOK NETWORK

British Library Cataloguing-in-Publication Information Available

Library of Congress Cataloging-in-Publication Data Available
ISBN 978-1-4930-2308-0 (paperback)
ISBN 978-1-4930-2309-7 (e-book)

∞™ The paper used in this publication meets the minimum requirements of American National Standard for Information Sciences—Permanence of Paper for Printed Library Materials, ANSI/NISO Z39.48-1992.

CONTENTS

Foreword by Rick Rinehart. v

Foreword by Mary Roberts Rinehart. xxi

ONE: The Adventurers. 1
TWO: "FALL IN". 7
THREE: The Sporting Chance 13
FOUR: All in the Game 21
FIVE: "Running Water and Still Pools" 27
SIX: The Call 31
SEVEN: The Black Marks. 39
EIGHT: Bears. 47
NINE: Down the Flathead Rapids. 53

About the Author 57

Foreword

The Spring of 1915 found Mary Roberts Rinehart in what we would nowadays call a funk. Recently returned from the battlefields of Europe, where she was the first correspondent of either sex or any nationality to visit The Front, she despaired of her return to the dull drumbeat of her life as mother, wife, and tireless writer. Moreover, she was preparing articles about her wartime experience for *The Saturday Evening Post*[1], a daily reminder of the horror she had witnessed across the Atlantic just a few weeks prior.

Then, like Peter Pan, in swept fellow Pittsburgher and newly minted rancher and trailblazer Howard Eaton, who took her to what was to become her Neverland: the American West. Furs, gowns, and feathered hats soon gave way to chaps, vests, and boots as the West gradually came to create an alter ego for the matronly and prim author. (As she remarked through one of her recurring characters, Letitia Carberry, "I've felt for a long time that I'd be glad to discard skirts. Skirts are badges of servitude, survivals of the harem, reminders of a time when nothing was expected of women but parasitic leisure.") Indeed, Howard Eaton's ranch in the Bighorn Mountains of Wyoming would become her summer home for decades to follow, the urban gloom of her youth but a distant, unhappy memory.

---

1 Collected later that year and published as *Kings, Queens, and Pawns: An American Woman at the Front* by George H. Doran. It has recently been reprinted by Taylor Trade Publishing (2015).

v

—◆—

Mary Ella Roberts was born in Allegheny, Pennsylvania, now a part of Pittsburgh, in 1876, in what has traditionally been referred to as "genteel poverty." "All week the house was busy enough, although there was no money," she wrote of her early childhood in a family cluster that consisted of her grandmother, Aunt Sade and Uncle John, as well as her own parents. "There never was any money in those days." Her father Tom was a dreamer, ostensibly the proprietor of a sewing machine shop, but in his heart an inventor whose several patents were "paid for in agony . . . later lapsing without result to him." Maybe in spite of himself, the business nevertheless prospered—briefly. He moved his family to their own home in 1880; two years later he was managing the Domestic Sewing Machine Company in Pittsburgh. However, by 1887 he had lost his franchise as well as his job. The small family picked up and moved to a less expensive, more austere neighborhood; Tom took to the road to sell everything from wallpaper to insurance policies.

Mary graduated from high school at the height of the Panic of 1893, fully expecting to pursue a career in medicine. However, the Panic changed all that: " . . . now when I spoke of going to college there was a curious silence," she later recalled. "My music lessons ceased. One day I came home to find that my belongings had been shifted to my sister's room on the second floor, and that two strange men had rented the room on the third." At about this time she submitted three short stories to the local newspaper in an effort to improve the household finances. All three were accepted for the disappointing sum of $1 each, after which she declared that her career as a woman of letters was over. Prophetically, however, her Uncle John remarked that there was enough plot in one of the stories to make a book.

Medicine still intrigued her, though, so she lied about her age and talked her way into Pittsburgh Training School for Nurses at Homeopathic Hospital in August of 1893, a place where surgeons who had learned their trade during the Civil War still insisted that maggots could be used to cleanse a dirty wound. Her first assignment was to remove from the operating room a bucket containing a human foot. Though this incident certainly shocked her, it did not make her physically ill. She reckoned at that moment that she was not only cut out for nursing but also the greater dramas in life. In her autobiography, *My Story*, she wrote:

> *And the emergency ward had drama. One morning I came on duty to find the battered body of a man who had been beaten to death with an iron pipe. One cold evening that fall just before going off duty, I turned down the bed for a burly policeman, crying as though his heart would break, while he placed on it the body of a small newsboy, burned and dying from the fire he had built to keep himself warm. A woman was brought in slashed in thirty places by a jealous rival with a knife; a pretty woman. She recovered.*

Indeed, her acceptance of the horror of life at such a tender age well-prepared her for the dreadful conditions on the Belgian Front years later. While her mysteries and romances may have been breezy and circumspect, her work as a journalist was at times direct and unrelenting. As she herself affirmed, "Why all the evasion, the fear of acknowledging what we know exists, goes on? A big emergency hospital deals with life itself. It cannot evade."

In her early days at the hospital she also became acquainted with the "rather severe" Dr. Stanley Marshall Rinehart, whose legendary scowl frightened away just about every nurse except the steely Mary Roberts. Dr. Rinehart, a very young (25 years old in 1894) surgeon and thus probably not of the maggots-as-antiseptic school, was known not only for his skill with the knife but also his perfectionism and fierce temper. However, Mary saw another side to him that clearly attracted her to him, because it was something that she so lacked as a weary and overworked nurse:

I was in the children's ward, and he had some cases there. More than that, he loved children. He would walk in, apparently very severe, looking through his pince-nez at the children, and they would rush to him and surround him. He was very gentle with them, and he would play with them. It seemed very strange to me, that playing. Neither then nor later had I that gift of being a child with children. . . . Later on when my own children were born I was to look back with much heart searching at the neat tidy machine which had fed and bathed and nursed those little wrecks of humanity. I had missed something there. But I was always tired . . .

Their acquaintance grew into a friendship; their friendship into a romance. Ever the risk-taker, Mary flouted hospital policy by agreeing to an engagement with a fellow staff member. Very soon thereafter the hospital's chief engineer stumbled upon a tryst and word spread like an epidemic. Confronted with the facts by the hospital board, Dr. Rinehart responded to their accusations by yelling at them and telling them that it was none of their business. With the meek request that Mary not flaunt her engagement by wearing a ring, the board simply "went away."

It was to be a two-year engagement, interrupted by a personal tragedy that Mary seemed to react to with disturbing detachment, even nearly forty years after the incident—which she recalled, almost as an anecdote, in *My Story*. Long despondent over his own failures as well as those precipitated by the nation's continued economic depression, Tom Roberts had shot himself through the heart and died while on a business trip to Buffalo on November 14, 1895. Away from the hospital and caring for a woman left alone with her illegitimate daughter to die of cancer, Mary received a telegram bearing the news. "It stunned me," she simply said of her response. The balance of the detail imparted in *My Story* is merely clinical:

> *Early the next morning I bought a paper to see if there was any explanation. There was indeed. It was blazoned on the front page. He had gone to a hotel in Buffalo and killed himself. Shot himself.*
>
> *I had not even known he owned a revolver.*

Indeed, prior to recounting the circumstances surrounding her father's suicide, she had shown more compassion defending the cancerous mother and her love child against the people who had ostracized them both:

She had had a child, and had had the courage to acknowledge it, so she was dying alone. Ever since that time, I have felt the cruelty and bitterness of our attitude toward the unmarried mother and her child. How stupid we are, that two wrongs can ever make a right.

Although later in life her politics could only be described as conservative, she showed a tendency—illustrated by these two events—to elevate the disenfranchised who accepted life as it was and met it head on over those who, notwithstanding the opportunities available to them, were confounded by it. In short, she did not abide weakness, most especially in herself. Unlike her father, she made no excuses.

Mary Ella Roberts became Mary Roberts Rinehart on April 21, 1896, and after intervals of illness and residual exhaustion brought on from her two years of work at the hospital, found my grandfather forming in her belly in December of that year. While none of her three pregnancies was easy, all three were ultimately successful, yielding first Stanley Marshall Rinehart, Jr. in 1897; then Alan Gillespie Rinehart in 1900; and finally Frederick Roberts Rinehart (Ted) two years later. By all accounts, both of her own hand as well as those of her biographers, marital life and motherhood did not comprise the crowning achievements of her life. "Once again, however, the world was a small place," she told readers in *My Story*, "smaller than ever." She further complained that she didn't dine out for ten years (because of Dr. Rinehart's late office hours) or sleep the night through for seven (because the boys apparently kept no particular hours).

There were moments of true crisis, however, that fully engaged her attention as wife, mother, and, working with her husband, medical practitioner. When Ted became gravely ill at six months and "solemn processions" of medical men would only shake their heads and go away, Dr. and Mrs. Rinehart would stare them down and will their child to live. He did. A year later, after he had swallowed enough carbolic acid to sicken a grown man, Ted again was given up for gone. In the family mythology, at least as my father tells it, Ted was in fact presumed deceased at one point following this incident and laid to rest (if temporarily). His sudden gurgling and crying told his parents he was not quite ready to be taken. Uncle Ted lived on to become a favorite of my father's (thus our common name, Frederick), and except for a bout with alcoholism, lived a long, loving, and exuberant life.

In 1904 the Rineharts were riding high with a house full of children and servants, a busy medical practice, and a stock portfolio worth $12,000. In her spare minutes Mary would dash off a few lines of verse and shop them around to popular magazines such as *Munsey's* and the Pittsburgh *Sunday Gazette*, where she published for the first time under the name of Mary Roberts Rinehart. On a visit to New York to try to sell a collection of her poems, she and Dr. Rinehart decided to pay a visit to the Stock Exchange for a firsthand look at how their money was growing. Instead, they witnessed a panic of the first order and came home knowing that their entire savings had been wiped out. Not only that, but they were $12,000 in debt as well. ("We might as well have owed twelve million," she wrote.) And even though Dr. Rinehart received a salary as city physician (and presumably a small stipend for representing the state board of health in the county), patient fees for an office visit were only $2 with perhaps an additional dollar for an office prescription. The practice of medicine was not then the lucrative profession that it has become today, and though Stan Rinehart earned more than most, every dime went to support the household—even after, "save one strong girl," all the servants were dismissed.

But this was not a precipitous ledge with a view to a deeper despair; it was the foot of the arc of a life that would make Mary Roberts Rinehart a household name in just a few years' time. Mary Roberts Rinehart was no Tom Roberts: faced with adversity, she declared that she "had found a way to help" the family after a short story was accepted by *Munsey's* for the sum of $34. And they wanted more:

> *I began to work now, to write fast and furiously, to listen with a sinking heart to the postman, to glance at the mail in a maid's hands and know at an incredible distance the envelope containing a returned manuscript. Now and then one was accepted. The checks at first were small, from ten to thirty dollars, but money was not important. I was learning a new profession, and being paid while I learned.*

By the middle of 1906 she had sold forty-six stories and made $1,842.50.

Notwithstanding the presence of a muse in her life, she did not succumb to the sort of creative self-indulgence that has isolated so many artists from their families, and ultimately broken them. She was fiercely devoted to her family and claimed in her autobiography that she would never work when the boys were in the house: "the slam of the front door" and "the shout of 'Mother' was the signal to stop." Except for slipping away for an hour or so under pressure of a deadline, she early on established a routine that did not allow her work to interfere with family life.

Still, possibly because she was exploring uncharted terrain for a woman of the early twentieth century, she did a bit of hair-splitting when it came to defending exactly what it was she was doing in those hours alone in the house. While freely referring to writing as her "profession," she refused to admit that it was a "career." Years later, when her reputation as a writer was well established, she wrote:

I did not want a career. The word has never been used in the family and never will be. I "work" when and where I can, but there is no real career, and never has been.

Webster's simple definition of *career* is "course of life"; for *profession* it is "a calling or occupation." By these narrow terms she differentiated her craft from that of writers who would sacrifice everything for the greater interests of their art. In retrospect, she was true to her ethos—at least as far as writing goes. Inadvertently, however, she did make a career out of something else, and that was building and promoting the American institution that she herself became. The emotional

sacrifices made by her family for the greater good of the institution were, at times, equal to those of any relative who has
lived in the penumbra of a personality who belonged to the
public as much as she belonged to her husband and children.

The cornerstone for this particular institution was laid
toward the end of the first decade of the new century, when,
at the urging of her Uncle John, she submitted a book-length
manuscript to a publisher. (Not knowing one publisher from
another, she picked one by the "simple method of taking a story
by Anna Katherine Green from the book case," and noted the
name. The fortunate imprint was Bobbs-Merrill in Indianapo-
lis.) Though intended as a satire of the mystery genre, *The Circular Staircase* was taken seriously by the critics, who stressed
the "relief of humor in a crime story." "I kept to myself," Mary
later recalled, "the deadly secret that the book had been writ-
ten as a semi-satire."

The Circular Staircase, which had sold 1.25 million copies,
was followed a year later by *The Man in the Lower Ten*, which
was the #4 bestseller in 1909, and *The Window at the White Cat*
and *When a Man Marries* as the #8 and #10 bestsellers in 1910.
The pattern continued pretty much unabated for the next
twenty-five years, with subsequent top-ten best-selling novels
in 1915, 1918, 1919, 1921, 1922, 1923, 1927, 1930, and 1936.
Indeed, when book club and paperback editions are taken into
account, Mary Roberts Rinehart was in all likelihood by 1950
the all-time best-selling fiction author in the United States
since the birth of the Republic.[2]

2 An article in the January 19, 1946, issue of *Publisher's Weekly* cited a list developed by
Irving Harlow Hart of the Iowa State Teachers College ranking the top 100 authors of
bestsellers in fiction from 1895 to 1944. Mary Roberts Rinehart led the list, followed

Howard Eaton's motive for inviting Rinehart out west was not entirely unselfish: he wanted to guide a party through newly established Glacier National Park in Montana during the summer of 1915, and he wanted it publicized. Since her novels and experience as a war correspondent had made Rinehart one of the most widely read (and trusted) authors in America, she was a natural for the job. As one of her biographers has noted, with the Eaton invitation "celebrityhood [had] bestowed its first gift." Initially hesitant because of work and family concerns, she at last agreed, believing that the West—still mysterious and partially unexplored—would give her great material for future articles. Since *The Saturday Evening Post* was not big on travel articles, she approached *Collier's*, which published her Glacier Park travelogue in two parts in April 1916.[3] Houghton Mifflin subsequently published the articles in a small book, *Through Glacier Park: Seeing America First with Howard Eaton*.[4]

---

by Winston Churchill. John Steinbeck ranked fifty-fourth and Ernest Hemingway ninety-sixth.

3 Another famous member of the Glacier party was Western artist Charlie Russell. A slightly lascivious letter from Russell, known to debauch every now and then after a few drinks, to Rinehart was discovered twenty years ago but has subsequently been lost.

4 An unexpected consequence of her trip to Montana was relief for the nearby Blackfeet tribe, which the government had forced into farming on barely arable land. Their cattle having been driven off by rustlers, the tribe suffered a famine during the winter of 1914-15. Encountering the "warrior woman" who had covered the Great War, they not only found someone who could help them but also made her an honorary member of the tribe. While Rinehart didn't shun the publicity that such an honor brought—she was given the name Pitamakin or "Running Eagle" and immediately notified her publisher's publicity department—she kept her promise with them. Upon returning East she stormed into Interior Secretary Franklin Lane's office and informed him of the humanitarian crisis in the West. Relief started flowing to the Blackfeet within days.

In the summer of 1916, clearly smitten by the West and its appeal to her adventurous side, she organized two trips, this time with the full family in tow. The first, through the largely unknown west side of Glacier National Park, required wilderness training for two weeks with Howard Eaton in East Glacier, and concluded with shooting the rapids of the Flathead River as quite possibly the first people (or perhaps the first white people) to do so. The second trip was even more daunting: an expedition over "totally unknown country" in the Washington Cascades to Puget Sound, a trip that included a movie photographer as well as numerous guides and packers. The trip, as recounted by Rinehart in her book *Tenting To-Night* (1917), was, as described by her biographer Jan Cohn, "clearly much more arduous" than her Glacier trip of the previous year, even at times "foolhardy."

After the Cascades crossing Mary Roberts Rinehart had had enough of adventure, but the West still came calling every summer until a weak heart in her later years prevented her from recreating comfortably in the high altitude of Eaton's Ranch. The Ranch itself was the subject of much of her final travelogue of the West, *The Out Trail* (1923), appropriately dedicated to the memory of Howard Eaton, who had passed away in 1922. The book also contains an account of a trip to Arizona and New Mexico during summer, as well as that of a perilous trip into Mexico where Rinehart seems to have been planted by the War Department as a quasi-spy. Sensing this, the Mexican government provided her and her two companions with an "escort" of two officers and five enlisted men. Still, Rinehart wrote that she was "so loaded with ammunition that a substantial blow would have exploded me."

All three of Rinehart's western travelogues are illustrated with photographs, all of surprisingly good quality for their time—probably because a professional photographer was usually a member of the Rinehart party. Still, they capture Mary Roberts Rinehart totally at ease in nature, in stark contrast to the formal portraiture that constituted her publishers' publicity photos. Here she is seen sitting in a boat and drinking water out of a felt hat; tying a fly with the fly rod positioned across her knees; sitting on a log surrounded by her family while eating breakfast; riding slowly through a mountainside teeming with larkspur. As if to draw a fine line between her cosmopolitan life on the east coast and the more casual and transcendent lifestyle of the West, newspapers would often announce in their social columns her departure in a manner that suggested that she was going "off the grid" for a time: "News Item: Mrs. Rinehart has gone to her ranch in Wyoming to spend the summer."

A few words need to be said in conclusion to paint the full picture of who Mary Roberts Rinehart was, and what she was to our family as well as her millions of readers. From my point of view, I like to say that she made us all possible, while also setting an impossibly high bar for her descendants. She was a feminine version of a Horatio Alger character and lived a life that Jan Cohn has described as an "improbable fiction." (The phrase is derivative of a line in Shakespeare's *Twelfth Night*:

"If this were play'd upon a stage now, I could condemn it as an improbable fiction.") During the Hoover administration she was offered at least two ambassadorships, the first woman in the United States to be so honored. Believing that she could be more effective as a private citizen, she declined them both. She underwrote and helped found Farrar & Rinehart in 1928, for which she has received little credit. The publishing firm went on to become Rinehart and Company and later Holt, Rinehart, and Winston. And in a groundbreaking gesture to her largely female audience, a piece she wrote for *The Saturday Evening Post* in 1947 was arguably her most widely read essay. "I Had Cancer" detailed her personal ordeal with breast cancer and encouraged women to self-examine, a hitherto forbidden topic of discussion.

—〜—

Outside Sewickley, Pennsylvania, the grounds of Rinehart's former estate now comprise the Mary Roberts Rinehart Nature Park. While the park's creators are probably unaware of Rinehart's influence in promoting places such as Glacier and other public lands, it is all too fitting that a small plot in her name is similarly dedicated to enjoyment and appreciation of the natural world. For her such enjoyment was sensuous; fresh from her first visit to Glacier, she exuberantly recalled the sensations of her three-hundred-mile journey across the Rockies: "to feel the glow of muscles too long unused; to sleep on the ground at night and find it soft; to eat, not because it is time to eat, but because one's body is clamoring for food; to drink where every stream and river is pure and cold; to get close to the earth and see the stars—this is travel." And we are also left with this final admonition, which is as meaningful today as it was when Mary Roberts Rinehart first penned it 100 years ago:

"Go ride in the Rocky Mountains and save your soul."

Rick Rinehart
Essex, Connecticut
August 2015

Foreword by Mary Roberts Rinehart

There are many to whom new places are only new pictures. But, after much wandering, this thing I have learned, and I wish I had learned it sooner: that travel is a matter, not only of seeing, but of doing.

It is much more than that. It is a matter of new human contacts. It is not of places, but of people. What are regions but the setting for life? The desert, without its Arabs, is but the place that God forgot.

To travel, then, is to do, not only to see. To travel best is to be of the sportsmen of the road. To take a chance, and win; to feel the glow of muscles too long unused; to sleep on the ground at night and find it soft; to eat, not because it is time to eat, but because one's body is clamoring for food; to drink where every stream and river is pure and cold; to get close to the earth and see the stars—this is travel.

ONE

The Adventurers

THIS IS ABOUT A THREE-HUNDRED-MILE TRIP ACROSS THE Rocky Mountains on horseback with Howard Eaton. It is about fishing, and cool nights around a camp-fire, and long days on the trail. It is about a party of all sorts, from everywhere, of men and women, old and young, experienced folk and novices, who had yielded to a desire to belong to the sportsmen of the road. And it is by way of being advice also. Your true convert must always preach.

If you are normal and philosophical; if you love your country; if you like bacon, or will eat it anyhow; if you are willing to learn how little you count in the eternal scheme of things; if you are prepared, for the first day or two, to be able to locate every muscle in your body and a few extra ones that seem to have crept in and are crowding, go ride in the Rocky Mountains and save your soul.

If you are of the sort that must have fresh cream in its coffee, and its steak rare, and puts its hair up in curlers at night, and likes to talk gossip in great empty places, don't go. Don't read this. Sit in a moving-picture theater and do your traveling.

But if you go—!

It will not matter that you have never ridden before. The horses are safe and quiet. The Western saddle is designed to keep a cow-puncher in his seat when his rope is around an infuriated steer. Fall off! For the first day or two, dear traveler, you will have to be extracted! After that you will learn that swing of the right leg which clears the saddle, the slicker, a camera, night-clothing, soap, towel, toothbrush, blanket, sweater, fishing-rod, fly-hook, comb, extra boots, and sunburn lotion, and enables you to alight in a vertical position and without jarring your spine up into your skull.

Now and then the United States Government does a very wicked thing. Its treatment of the Indians, for instance, and especially of the Blackfeet, in Montana. But that's another story. The point is that, to offset these lapses, there are occasional Government idealisms. Our National Parks are the expression of such an ideal.

I object to the word "park," especially in connection with the particular National Reserve in northwestern Montana known as Glacier Park. A park is a civilized spot, connected in all our minds with neat paths and clipped lawns. I am just old enough to remember when it meant "Keep-Off-the-Grass" signs also, and my childhood memories of the only park I knew are inseparably connected with a one-armed policeman with a cane and an exaggerated sense of duty.

There are no "Keep-Off-the-Grass" signs in Glacier Park, no graveled paths and clipped lawns. It is the wildest part of America. If the Government had not preserved it, it would have preserved itself. No homesteader would ever have invaded its rugged magnificence or dared its winter snows. But you and I would not have seen it.

True, so far most niggardly provision has been made. The Government offices are a two-roomed wooden cabin. The national warehouse is a barn. To keep it up, to build trails and roads, to give fire protection for its fourteen hundred square miles of great forest, with many millions of dollars' worth of timber, are provided thirteen rangers! Thirteen rangers, and an annual allowance less than half of what is given to Yellowstone Park,—with this difference, too, that Yellowstone Park has had money spent on it for thirty-two years while Glacier Park is in the making! It is one of the merry little jests we put over now and then. For seventy-five miles in the north of the park there is no ranger. Government property, you see, and no protection.

But no niggardliness on the part of the Government can cloud the ideal which is the raison d'être for Glacier Park. Here is the last stand of the Rocky Mountain sheep, the Rocky Mountain goat. Here are antelope and deer, black and grizzly bears, mountain lions, trout—well, we are coming to the trout. Here are trails that follow the old game trails along the mountain-side; here are meadows of June roses, true forget-me-nots, larkspur, Indian paintbrush, fireweed,—that first plant to grow after forest fires,—a thousand sorts of flowers, growing beside snow-fields. Here are ice and blazing sun, vile roads, and trails of a beauty to make you gasp.

A congressional committee went out to Glacier Park in 1914 and three of their machines went into the ditch. They went home and voted a little money for roads after that, out of gratitude for their lives. But they will have to vote more money, much more money, for roads. A Government mountain reserve without plenty of roads is as valuable as an automobile without gasoline.

Nevertheless,—bad roads or good or none, thirteen rangers or a thousand,—seen from an automobile or from a horse, Glacier Park is a good place to visit. Howard Eaton thinks so. Last July, with all of the West to draw from, he took his first party through Glacier. This year in June, with his outfit on a pack-horse, he is going to investigate some new trails and in July he will take a party of riders over them.

Forty-two people set out with Howard Eaton last summer to ride through Glacier Park. They were of every age, weight, and temperament. About half were women. But one thing they had in common—the philosophy of true adventure.

Howard Eaton is extremely young. He was born quite a number of years ago, but what is that? He is a boy, and he takes an annual frolic. And, because it means a cracking good time, he takes people with him and puts horses under them and the fear of God in their hearts, and bacon and many other things, including beans, in their stomachs.

He has taken foreign princes and many of the great people of the earth to the tops of high mountains, and shown them grizzly bears, and their own insignificance, at one and the same time. He is a hunter, a sportsman, and a splendid gentleman. And, because equipment is always a matter of much solicitude on the part of the novice, I shall tell you what he wears when, on his big horse, he leads his long line of riders over the trails. He wears a pair of serviceable trousers, a blue shirt, and a vest! Worn by Howard Eaton, believe me, they are real clothes.

He has hunted along the Rockies from Alaska to Mexico. He probably knows Montana, Wyoming, and Idaho as well as any man in the country.

When Howard Eaton first went West he located in the Bad Lands. Those were the "buffalo" days, and it was then that he began taking his friends with him on hunting trips. At first they went as his guests. Even now they are his guests in the truest sense of the word.

By their own insistence, as the parties grew larger, they determined to help defray the cost of the expeditions. Every one who knows Howard Eaton knows that his trips are not made for profit. Probably they barely pay for themselves. It is impossible to talk to him about money. Save as a medium of exchange it does not exist for him. Life for him is twenty-four hours in the open air,—half of that time in the saddle,—long vistas, the trail of game, the camp-fire at night, and a few hours of quiet sleep under the stars.

Roosevelt's ranch was near the Eaton ranch when it was in the Bad Lands. Roosevelt and Howard Eaton have taken many hunting trips together. Titled foreigners of all sorts have come over and hunted elk, deer, and other game with him. He has supplied museums, parks, and animal shows in every part of America with game. He was and is a crack shot, of course. He says he always treated the Indians with respect. "I was always a little shy when Indians were in the same country with me, and once when hunting I retired so fast that the boys said I beat my shadow six miles in fifteen minutes."

In those days the town of Sentinel Butte consisted of a canvas saloon with the sign:—

Rev. C. A. Duffy
Best Wines, Liquors, and Cigars

"I had a fine chance to steal that sign once," says Howard Eaton, "but some folks are fools, and I overlooked a bet."

The Eaton "boys"—for there are three—left Pittsburg and went West many years ago. Howard was the first. He went in 1879. In 1884 Theodore Roosevelt went out to the same country. It was in 1904 when the Eatons left the Bad Lands and went toward the Big Horn Mountain. There, at the foot of Wolf Creek and in the center of the historic battle-ground of the Arapahoes, Sioux, Crows, and Cheyennes, they established a new ranch at Wolf, Wyoming.

Two

"FALL IN"

The rendezvous for the Eaton party last summer was at Glacier Park Station on the Great Northern Railway. Getting to that point, remote as it seemed, had been surprisingly easy—almost disappointingly easy. Was this, then, going to the borderland of civilization, to the last stronghold of the old West? Over the flat country, with inquiring prairie dogs sitting up to inspect us, the train of heavy Pullman diners and club car moved steadily toward the purple drop-curtain of the mountains. West, always west.

Now and then we stopped, and passengers got on. They brought with them something new, rather electric. It was enthusiasm. The rest, who had been Eastern and greatly bored, roused and looked out of the windows. For the newcomers were telling fairy tales, with wheat for gold and farmers for princes, and backing everything with figures. They think in bushels over rather a large part of America to-day.

West. Still west. An occasional cowboy silhouetted against the sky; thin range cattle; impassive Indians watching the train go by; a sawmill, and not a tree in sight over a vast horizon! Red raspberries as large as strawberries served in the diner, and trout from the mountains that seemed no nearer by mid-day than at dawn!

Then, at last, at twilight, Glacier Park Station, and Howard Eaton on the platform, and old Chief Three Bears, of the Blackfeet, wonderfully dressed and preserved at ninety-three.

It was rather a picturesque party. Those who had gone up from the Eaton ranch in Wyoming—a trifle of seven hundred miles—wore their riding-clothes to save luggage. Khaki was the rule, the women mostly in breeches and long coats, with high-laced shoes reaching to the knee and soft felt hats, the men in riding-clothes, with sombreros and brilliant bandannas knotted about their throats. One or two had rather overdone the part and were the objects of good-natured chaffing later on by the guides and cowboys.

"Hi!" cried an urchin as we walked about the streets of Billings, Montana, to stretch train-tired muscles. "Here's the 101 Ranch!"

Not very long before I had been to the front in Belgium and in France. I confess that no excursion to the trenches gave me a greater thrill than the one that accompanied that start the next morning from the Glacier Park Hotel to cross the Continental Divide. For we were going to cross the Rockies. Our route was three hundred miles long. It was over six passes, and if you believe, as I did, that a pass is a valley between two mountains, I am here to set you right.

A pass is a bloodcurdling spot up which one's horse climbs like a goat and down the other side of which it slides as you lead it, trampling ever and anon on a tender part of your foot. A pass is the highest place between two peaks. A pass is not an opening, but a barrier which you climb with chills and descend with prayer. A pass is a thing which you try to forget at the time and which you boast about when you get back home. For I have made it clear, I think, that a horseback trip through Glacier Park, across the Rockies, and down the Pacific Slope, is a sporting proposition. It is safe enough. Howard Eaton has never had an accident. But there are times—

Once, having left the party to make a side trip, my precious buckskin horse—called "Gold Dollar"—was "packed" over. Now, Gold Dollar was a real horse with a beard. He was not a handsome horse. Even when I was on him, no one would have turned to admire. But he was a strong horse, and on a trail up a switchback—do you know what a switchback is?—well, a mountain switchback bears about as much relation to the home-grown amusement-park variety as a stepmother to the real thing—on a switchback he was well-behaved. He hugged the inside of the trail, and never tried to reach over the edge, with a half-mile drop below, to crop grass. He was not reckless. He was a safe and sane horse. He never cared for me, but that is beside the question.

So, having temporarily left Gold Dollar, I had to get back to him. I had to go fifty miles to do it, and I was provided with a horse by the man who holds the horse concession in the park. A horse? A death-trap, a walking calamity, a menace. If the companies who carry my life insurance had seen me on that horse, they would have gone pale. He was a white horse, and he was a pack-horse. Now, the way of a pack-horse is on the edge of the grave. Because of his pack he walks always at the outer side of the trail. If his pack should happen to hit the rocky wall, many unpleasant things would follow, including buzzards. So this beast, this creature, this steed of death, walked on the edge of the precipice. He counted that moment lost that saw not two feet dangling blithely over the verge. Now and then the verge crumbled. We dislodged large stones that fell for a mile or two, with a sickening thud. Once we crossed a snow-field which was tilted. He kept one foot on the trail and gave the other three a chance to take a slide. There was a man riding behind me. When it was all over, he shook my hand.

Off, then, to cross the Rocky Mountains—forty-two of us, and two wagons which had started early to go by road to the first camp: cowboys in chaps and jingling spurs; timorous women, who eyed rather askance the blue and purple mountains back of the hotel; automobile tourists, partly curious and partly envious; the inevitable photographer, for whom we lined up in a semi-circle, each one trying to look as if starting off on such a trip was one of the easiest things we did; and over all the bright sun, a breeze from the mountains, and a sense of such exhilaration as only altitude and the West can bring.

Then a signal to fall in. For a mile or two we went two abreast, past a village of Indian tepees, past meadows scarlet with the Indian paintbrush, past—with condescension—automobile busses loaded with tourists who craned and watched. Then to the left, and off the road. The cowboys and guides were watching us. As we strung out along the trail, they rode back and forward, inspecting saddles, examining stirrups, seeing that all were comfortable and safe. For even that first day we were to cross Mount Henry, and there must be no danger of saddle slipping.

Quite without warning we plunged into a rocky defile, with a small river falling in cascades. The shadow of the mountain enveloped us. The horses forded the stream and moved sedately on.

Did you ever ford a mountain stream on horseback? Do it. Ride out of the hot sun into a brawling valley. Watch your horse as he feels his way across, the stream eddying about his legs. Give him his head and let him drink lightly, skimming the very surface of the water with his delicate nostrils. Lean down and fill your own cup. How cold it is, and how clear! Uncontaminated it flows down from the snow-covered mountains overhead. It is living.

Three

The Sporting Chance

The trail began to rise to the tree-covered "bench." It twisted as it rose. Those above called cheerfully to those below. We had settled to the sedate walk of our horses, the pace which was to take us over our long itinerary. Hardly ever was it possible, during the days that followed, to go faster than a walk. The narrow, twisting trails forbade it. Now and then a few adventurous spirits, sighting a meadow, would hold back until the others had got well ahead, and then push their horses to the easy Western lope. But such joyous occasions were rare.

Up and up. The trail was safe, the grade easy. At the edge of the bench we turned and looked back. The great hotel lay below in the sunlight. Leading to it were the gleaming rails of the Great Northern Railway. We turned our horses and went on toward the snow-covered peaks ahead.

The horses moved quietly, one behind the other. As the trail rose there were occasional stops to rest them. Women who had hardly dared to look out of a third-story window found themselves on a bit of rocky shelf, with the tops of the tallest trees far below. The earth, as we had known it, was falling back. And, high overhead, Howard Eaton, at the head of the procession, was sitting on his big horse silhouetted against the sky.

The first day was to be an easy one—twelve miles and camp. "Twelve miles!" said the experienced riders. "Hardly a Sunday morning canter!" But a mountain mile is a real mile. Possibly they measure from peak to peak. I do not know. I do know that we were almost six hours making that twelve miles and that for four of it we led our horses down a mountain-side over a vacillating path of shale. Knees, that up to that point had been fairly serviceable, took to chattering. Riding-boots ceased to be a matter of pride and emerged skinned and broken. The horses slid and stumbled. And luncheon receded.

Down and down! Great granite cliffs of red and blue and yellow across the valley—and no luncheon! Striped squirrels hiding in the shale—and no luncheon! A great glow of moving blood through long-stagnant vessels, deep breaths of clear mountain air, a camera dropped on the trail, a stone in a horse's foot—and no luncheon!

Two o'clock, and we were down. The nervous woman who had never been on a horse before was cinching her own saddle and looking back and up. The saddle tightened, she sat down and emptied her riding-boots of a few pieces of rock. Her silk stockings were in tatters.

"I feel as though my knees will never meet again," she said reflectively. "But I'm so swollen with pride and joy that I could shriek."

That's what it is, partly. A sense of achievement; of conquering the unconquerable; of pitting human wits against giants and winning—a sporting chance. You may climb peaks in a railroad coach and see things as wonderful. But you are doing this thing yourself. Every mile is an achievement. And, after all, it is miraculously easy. The trails are good. The horses are steady and sure-footed. It is a triumph of endurance rather than of courage.

If you have got this far, you are one of us, and you will go on. For the lure of the high places is in your blood. The call of the mountains is a real call. The veneer, after all, is so thin. Throw off the impedimenta of civilization, the telephones, the silly conventions, the lies that pass for truth. Go out to the West. Ride slowly, not to startle the wild things. Throw out your chest and breathe; look across green valleys to wild peaks where mountain sheep stand impassive on the edge of space. Let the summer rains fall on your upturned face and wash away the memory of all that is false and petty and cruel. Then the mountains will get you. You will go back. The call is a real call.

Above the timber-line we rode along bare granite slopes. Erosion had been busy here. The mighty winds that sweep the crests of the Rockies had bared the mountains' breasts. Beside the trails high cairns of stones were piled, so that during the winter snow the rangers might find their way about. Remember, this is northwestern Montana; the Canadian border is only a few miles away, and over these peaks sweeps the full force of the great blizzards of the Northwest.

The rangers keep going all winter. There is much to be done. In the summer it is forest fires and outlaws. In the winter there are no forest fires, but there are poachers after mountain sheep and goats, opium smugglers, bad men from over the Canadian border. Now and then a ranger freezes to death. All summer these intrepid men on their sturdy horses go about armed with revolvers. But in the fall—snow begins early in September, sometimes even in August—they take to snowshoes. With a carbine strung to his shoulders, matches in a waterproof case, snowshoes and a package of food in his pocket, the Glacier Park ranger covers unnumbered miles, patrolling the wildest and most storm-ridden country in America. He travels alone. The imprint of a strange snowshoe on the trail rouses his suspicion. Single-handed he follows the marks in the snow. A blizzard comes. He makes a wikiup of branches, lights a small fire, and plays solitaire until the weather clears. The prey he is stalking cannot advance either. Then one day the snow ceases; the sun comes out. Over the frozen crust his snowshoes slide down great slopes with express speed. Generally he takes his man in. Sometimes the outlaw gets the drop on the ranger first and gets away.

During the winter of 1913 one of these rangers was frozen to death. He was caught in a blizzard, and he knew what was coming. When at last he sat down beside the trail to wait for death he placed his snowshoes points upward in the snow beside him. He sat there, and the snow came down and covered him. They found him the next day by the points of his snowshoes.

The snow melts in the summer on the meadows and in the groves. But the peaks are still covered, and here and there the trail leads through a snow-field. The horses venture out on it gingerly. The hot sun that blisters the face seems to make no impression on these glacier-like patches, snow on top and ice beneath. Flowers grow at their very borders. Striped squirrels and whistling marmots, much like Eastern woodchucks, run about, quite fearless, or sit up and watch the passing of the line of horses and riders, so close that they can almost be touched.

Great spaces; cool, shadowy depths in which lie blue lakes; mountain-sides threaded with white, where, from some hidden lake or glacier far above, the overflow falls a thousand feet or more, and over all the great silence of the Rockies! Nerves that have been tightened for years slowly relax. There is not much talking. The horses move along slowly. The sun beats down. Some one, shading his eyes with his hand, proclaims a mountain sheep or goat on a crag overhead. The word passes back along the line. Also a thrill. Then some wretched electrical engineer or college youth or skeptical lawyer produces a pair of field-glasses and announces it to be a patch of snow.

Here and there we saw "tourist goats," rocks so shaped and situated as to defy the strongest glass. The guides pointed them out and listened with silent enjoyment to the resulting acclamation. After that discovery, we adopted a safe rule: nothing was a goat that did not move. Long hours we spent while our horses wandered on with loose reins, our heads lifted to that line, just above the timber, which is Goatland. And the cry "A goat!" and the glasses, and skepticism—often undeserved.

The first night out of doors I did not sleep. I had not counted on the frosty nights, and I was cold. The next day I secured from a more provident member of the party woolen pajamas. Clad in those, and covered with all the extra portions of my wardrobe, I was more comfortable. But it takes woolen clothing and bed socks to keep out the chill of those mountain nights.

One rises early with Howard Eaton's party. No matter how late the story-tellers have held the crowd the night before around the camp-fire, somewhere about five o'clock, Howard—he is either Howard or Uncle Howard to everybody—comes calling among the silent tepees.

"Time to get up!" he calls. "Five o'clock and a fine morning. Up with you!"

And everybody gets up. There are basins about. Each one clutches his cake of soap and his towel, and fills his basin from whatever lake or stream is at hand. There is plenty of water in Glacier Park, and the camps are generally beside a lake. The water is cold. It ought to be, being glacier water, cold and blue. The air is none too warm. A few brave spirits seek isolation and a plunge bath. The majority are cowards.

Now and then a luxurious soul worried the cook for hot water. They tell of a fastidious lady who carried a small tin pail of water to the cook tent and addressed the cook nervously as he beat the morning flapjacks with a savage hand.

"Do you think," she inquired nervously, "if—if I put this water on your stove, it will heat?"

He turned and eyed her.

"You see it's like this, lady," he said. "My father was a poor man and couldn't give me no education. Damned if I know. What do you think?"

Before one is fairly dressed, with extra garments thrust into the canvas war-sack or duffle-bag which is each person's allowance for luggage, the tents are being taken down and folded. The cook comes to the end of the big tent.

"Come and get it!" he yells through hollowed hands.

"Come and get it!" is repeated down the line of tepees. That is the food call of an Eaton camp. Believe me, it has the butler's "Dinner is served, madame," beaten forty ways for Sunday. There is no second call. You go or you don't go. The long tables under the open end of the cook tent are laden with bacon, ham, fried eggs, flapjacks, round tins of butter, enameled cups of hot coffee, condensed milk, sometimes fried fish. For the cook can catch trout where the most elaborately outfitted Eastern angler fails.

The horses come in with a thudding of hoofs and are rounded up by the men into the rope corral. Watched by night herders, they have been grazing quietly all night in mountain valleys. There is not much grass for them. By the end of the three-hundred-mile trip they are a little thin, although in good condition. It is the hope of the Superintendent of the Park and of others interested that the Government will soon realize the necessity for planting some of the fertile valleys and meadows with grass. There are certain grasses that will naturalize themselves there—for instance, clover, blue-joint, and timothy. Beyond the first planting they would need nothing further. And, since much of the beauty of this park will always be inaccessible by motor, it can never be properly opened up until horses can get sufficient grazing.

Sometimes, at night, our horses ranged far for food,—eight miles,—even more. Again and again I have watched my own horse nosing carefully along a green bank and finding nothing at all, not a blade of grass it could eat.

With the second day came a new sense of physical well-being, and this in spite of a sunburn that had swollen my face like a toothache. Already telephones and invitations to dinner and tailor's fittings and face powder belonged to the forgotten past. I carried over my saddle and placed it beside my horse, and a kindly and patronizing member of Howard Eaton's staff put it on and cinched it for me. I never learned how to put the thing on, but I did learn, after a day or two, to take it off, as well as the bridle and the red hackamore, and then to stand clear while my buckskin pony lay down and rolled in the grass to ease his weary back. All the horses rolled, stiff-legged. If the saddle did not come off in time, they rolled anyhow, much to the detriment of cameras, field-glasses, and various impedimenta strapped thereon.

Four

All in the Game

Day after day we progressed. There were bright days and days when we rode through a steady mist of rain. Always it was worth while. What matters a little rain when there is a yellow slicker to put on and no one to care how one looks? Once, riding down a mountain-side, water pouring over the rim of my old felt hat and pattering merrily on my slicker, I looked to one side to see a great grizzly raise himself from behind a tree-trunk, and, standing upright, watch impassively as my horse and I proceeded. I watched him as far as I could see him. We were mutually interested. The party had gone on ahead. For a long time afterward I heard the crackling of small twigs in the heavy woods beside the trail. But I never saw him again.

It is strange to remember how little animal life, after all, there seemed to be. There was plenty, of course. But our party was large. We had no chance to creep up silently on the wild life of the park. The vegetation was so luxuriant in the valleys. Beyond an occasional bear, once or twice the screaming of a mountain lion, and the gophers and marmots, we saw nothing. There were not many birds. We never saw a snake. It was too high.

One day, riding along a narrow trail on a mountain-side, the horse in front of mine stampeded, and for a moment it looked like serious trouble. For a stampeding horse on a two-foot trail is a dangerous thing. It developed that there was a wasp's nest there, and the horse had been stung. We all got by finally by lashing our horses and running past at a canter.

Another time, working slowly up a mountain-side, I told the chief ranger of the park of having seen many Western horses at the front in France.

"Do you remember any of the brands?" he asked.

I did. A Diamond-Z, a flank brand on a black horse at Ypres.

"That's curious," he commented. "That man just ahead of us has shipped a carload of Montana horses to the front, and I believe that is his brand."

We called to the man ahead, and he halted. Up we rode and demanded his brand. It was the Diamond-Z. To be quite certain, he showed it to me registered in his notebook.

So there, where we could see out over what seemed unlimited space, where the earth appeared a vast thing, we decided that, after all, it was a small place. The Rocky Mountains and Ypres!

Having risen at five, by eleven o'clock thoughts of luncheon were always obtrusive. People began stealthily to consult watches and look ahead for a shady place to stop. By half-past eleven we were generally dismounted in some grove and the pack-train was coming up with its clattering pans, its coffee-pot, its cold boiled ham.

Howard Eaton always made the coffee. It was good coffee. Apparently nobody ever thought of tea. In the out-doors it is coffee—strong coffee, as hot as possible—that one craves.

There was one young woman in the party to whom things were always happening—not by her own fault. If there was a platter of meat to be dropped, it fell in her lap. And so I remember that one day, the coffee having been made at a luncheon stop, the handle came off the coffee-pot and this same young woman had an uncomfortable baptism.

But it was all in the game. Hot coffee, marmalade, bread and butter, cheese, sardines, and the best ham in the world— that was luncheon. Often there was a waterfall near, where for the mere holding out of a cup there was ice water to drink. The horses were not unsaddled at these noonday stops, but, having climbed hard all morning, they were glad to stand in the shade and rest.

Sometimes we lunched on a ledge where all the kingdoms of the earth seemed spread out before us. We sprawled on rocks, on green banks, and relaxed muscles that were weary with much climbing. There was much talk of a desultory sort. We settled many problems, but without rancor. The war was far away. Here were peace and a great contentment, food and a grassy bank, and overhead the trail called us to new vistas, new effort.

One young man was the party poet. He hit us all off sooner or later. I have the ode he wrote to me, but modesty forbids that I give it.

The poet having pocketed his pad and pencil, and the amateur photographers having put up their cameras, the order to start was given. The dishes were piled back in the crates and strapped to the pack-horses. The ruin of the ham was wrapped up and tied on somewhere. Dark glasses were adjusted against the glare, and we were off.

Sometimes our destination towered directly overhead, up a switchback of a trail where it was necessary to divide the party into groups, so that no stone dislodged by a horse need fall on some one below. Always at the head, riding calmly, with keen blue eyes, that are like the eyes of aviators and sailors in that they seem to look through long distances, was Howard Eaton. Every step of the trail he tested first, he and his big horse. And I dare say many a time he drew a breath of relief when the last timid woman had reached a summit or descended a slope or forded a river, and nothing untoward had happened.

There were days when we reached our camping-places by mid-afternoon. Then the anglers got their rods and started out for trout. There were baths to be taken in sunny pools that looked warm and were icy cold. There were rents in riding-clothes to be mended; even—whisper it—a little laundry work to be done now and then by women, some of them accustomed to the ministrations of a lady's maid at home. And there was supper and the camp-fire. Charley Russell, the cowboy artist, was the camp-fire star. To repeat one of his stories would be desecration. No one but Charley Russell himself, speaking through his nose, with his magnificent head outlined against the firelight, will ever be able to tell one of his stories.

There were other good story-tellers in the party. And Howard Eaton himself could match them all. A hundred miles from a railroad, we gathered around that camp-fire in the evening in a great circle. There were, you will remember, forty-two of us—no mean gathering. The pine and balsam crackled and burned, and overhead, often rising in straight walls around us for thousands of feet, were the snow-capped peaks of the Continental Divide. Little by little the circle would grow smaller until at last only a dozen choice spirits remained for a midnight debauch of anecdote.

I have said that the horses ranged wide at night. Occasionally they stayed about the camp. There was one big horse that was belled at night. Now and then toward dawn he brought his ungainly body, his tinkling bell, and his satellites, the other horses, into the quiet streets of tepee town. More than once I have seen an irate female, clad in pajamas and slippers, with flying braids, shooing the horses away from her tent in the gray, cold dawn, and flinging after them things for which she vainly searched the next morning.

FIVE

"Running Water and Still Pools"

HOLIDAYS ARE RARE WITH ME. SO, ON THOSE OCCASIONAL days when the party rested, I was up and away. I happen to like to fish. The same instinct which sent me as a child on my grandaunt's farm, armed with a carefully bent pin, an old cigar box full of worms, and a piece of twine, to sit for hours over a puddle in a meadow and fish for minnows; the same ambition which took me on flying feet up the hillside to deposit my prey, still wriggling, in a water barrel, where for days I offered it food in the shape of broken crackers, and wept to find eventually its little silver belly upturned to the morning sky—that joy of running water and still pools and fish is still mine.

I cannot cast for trout. I do it, but my technique sets the boat to rocking and fishermen to grinding their teeth.

But I had taken West with me a fly book and a trout rod, and I meant to use them. Now and then, riding along the trail, we met people who drew aside to let us pass, and who held up such trout as I had never dreamed of. Or, standing below a waterfall, would be a silent fisherman too engrossed to more than glance at our procession as it wound along.

But repeated early attempts brought me not a single strike. Once in my ardor I fell into an extremely cold lake and had to be dried out for hours. I grew caustic about the trout. Then somebody, with the interests of the park at stake, said that he would make up a party and see that I caught some trout. He would see that I caught something, he said, if he had to crawl into the lake and bite my hook himself.

So we went to Red Eagle Lake. There are trout in that lake; there are cutthroat trout weighing four pounds. I sat in a boat with a man who drew one in. I saw two college boys in their undergarments standing up to the waist in ice water and getting more large trout than I knew were in the world. I ate trout that other people caught. But they were bitter in my mouth.

I threatened to write up Glacier Park as being a fishing failure. The result was calamitous. Earnest-eyed fishermen spent hours in rowing me about. They imperiled my life, taking me into riffles; they made me brave pneumonia and influenza and divers other troubles in the determination that I should catch a mammoth fish. And nothing happened—nothing whatever. Once a man in the boat hooked a big one and it ran under the boat. I caught the line and jerked the fish into the boat. That was the nearest I came to catching a large cutthroat trout at Red Eagle Lake. Later on—but I haven't come to that yet.

I did catch some fish at Red Eagle. I caught some Dolly Varden and rainbow trout. One of the earnest fishermen led me on foot over several miles of Rocky Mountain scenery, stopping ever and anon to show me where a large bear had just passed. The trail was fresh. Here were the stones he had turned over for ants, the old trunks he had scratched for grubs. Then we arrived at the foot of a waterfall.

What a place it was! The water poured down in clouds of spray on which the afternoon sun painted a rainbow. Tiny water ouzels bathed and played in the pools in shallow rocks. And here, in deep holes, there were trout for the catching.

The fisherman stationed me on a rock, weighted my hook, told me to drop in about forty feet of line, and stand still. They would hook themselves. They did. I caught eight in fifteen minutes. But it was not sport. It was as interesting as fishing for gold-fish in an aquarium.

I lay that night at Red Eagle in a tent on a bed built of young trees driven into the ground and filled with balsam branches. A pack-horse had carried up the blankets and pillows. It was a couch for a queen. In the forest a mountain lion screamed like a woman, and at two o'clock in the morning one of the college boys got up from the cook tent where he was sleeping, and said he thought he would go fishing!

As I look back, that was a strange gathering at the fishing-camp at Red Eagle—so very far from anything approaching civilization. There was a moving-picture man and his outfit, there were the two college men, there was the chief ranger of Glacier Park. There was a young couple from New England who were tramping through the park, carrying their tent and other things on their backs. They were very young and very enthusiastic. I suspected them of being bride and groom, although I did not know, and the most vivid recollection I have is of seeing the young woman washing their camp-dishes in the cleanest, soapiest dishwater I had seen since I left home.

And there was a cook who is a business man in the winter, and who made excellent soda biscuit and talked books to me.

That night, around the camp-fire, there were more stories told. The college boys—"Pie" Way, the Yale pitcher, was one—related many marvelous tales. They said they were true. I hope so. If they were, life is even more interesting and thrilling a thing than I had believed. If they were fiction, they had me beaten at my own game.

The next day was lowering and cold. I spent the morning trying to get fish, and retired sour and disappointed when every one else succeeded and I failed. Sometime I am going back to Red Eagle Lake, and I shall take with me a tin of coral-colored salmon eggs—a trick I learned from George Locke on the Flathead River later on. And then I intend to have my photograph taken with strings of fish like bunches of bananas around me.

Six

The Call

As the days went on there was a subtle change in the party. Women, who had to be helped into their saddles at the beginning of the trip, swung into them easily. Waistbands were looser, eyes were clearer; we were tanned; we were calm with the large calmness of the great outdoors. And with each succeeding day the feeling of achievement grew. We were doing things and doing them without effort. To some of us the mountains had made their ancient appeal. Never again should we be clear of their call.

To those of us who felt all this inevitably in the future would come times when cities and even civilization itself would cramp.

I have traveled a great deal. The Alps have never held this lure for me. Perhaps it is because these great mountains are my own, in my own country. Cities call—I have heard them. But there is no voice in all the world so insistent to me as the wordless call of the Rockies. I shall go back. Those who go once always hope to go back. The lure of the great free spaces is in their blood.

We crossed many passes. Dawson Pass was the first difficult Rocky Mountain pass I had ever seen. There was a time when I had thought that a mountain pass was a depression. It is not. A mountain pass is a place where the impossible becomes barely possible. It is a place where wild game has, after much striving, discovered that it may get from one mountain valley to another. Along these game trails men have built new paths. Again and again we rode through long green valleys, the trail slowly rising until it had left timber far below. Then at last we confronted a great rock wall, a seemingly impassable barrier. Up this, by infinite windings, back and forward went the trail. At the top was the pass.

"I'm getting right tired," said Charley Russell, "of standing in a cloud up to my waist."

Each new pass brought a new vista of blue distance, of white peaks. Each presented its own problems of ascent or descent. No two were alike. Mountain-climbing is like marriage. Whatever else it may be, it is always interesting.

There was the day we went over the Cutbank Pass, with instructions to hold our horses' manes so that our saddles would not slip back. I shall never forget my joy at reaching the summit and the horror that followed when I found I was on a rocky wall about twenty feet wide which dropped a half-mile straight down on the other side to a perfectly good blue lake. There was Triple Divide. There was the Piegan Pass, where, having left the party for a time, I rode back to them on the pack-horse I have mentioned before, with my left foot dangling over eternity.

Triple Divide. The trail had just been completed, and ours was the first party after the trail-makers. I had expected to be the first woman on the top of Triple Divide. But when I arrived, panting and breathless and full of the exaltation of the moment, two girls were already there sitting on a rock. I shall not soon recover from the indignant surprise of that moment. Perhaps they never knew that they had taken the laurel wreath from my brow.

Triple Divide is really the culminating point of the continent. It is called Triple Divide because water flows from it into the Gulf of Mexico, into the Pacific Ocean, and into Hudson Bay.

There was the day when, on our way to Gunsight, we rode for hours along a trail that heavy rains had turned into black swamp. The horses struggled, constantly mired. It was the hardest day of the trip, not because of the distance, which was only thirty-five miles, but on account of the constant rocking in the saddle as our horses wallowed out of one "jack pot" into another—jack pots, I presume, because they are easy to get into and hard to get out of!

There was some grunting when at the end of that day we fell out of our saddles, but no complaining. That night, for the first time, the Eaton party slept under a roof at the Gunsight Chalet, on the shores of a blue lake. The Blackfoot Glacier was almost overhead. It was the end of a hot July, but we gathered around a fire that evening, and crawled in under heavy blankets to the quick sleep of fatigue.

One more pass, and we should be across the Rockies and moving down the Pacific Slope. The moon came up that night and shone on the ice-caps of the mountains all around us, on the glacier, on the Gunsight itself, appropriately if not beautifully named. As far up the mountain-side as the glacier our tired horses ranged for grass, and the tiny fire of the herder made a red glow that disappeared as the night mist closed down.

No "Come and get it" the next morning, but a good breakfast, nevertheless: a frosty morning, with the sun out, and the moving-picture man gone ahead to catch us as we climbed. There was another photographer who had joined the party. He had been up at dawn, on the chance of snapping a goat or two.

Late the next night, when after a hard day's ride we had reached civilization again at Lake Macdonald, and had dined and rested, the ambitious young man limped into the hotel on foot. For more than twenty miles he had tramped, carrying a heavy plate camera and extra plates. The zeal of the artist had made him careless. He left his horse untied, and it promptly followed the others.

Of the last part of that trip of his afoot I do not care to think. The trail, having scaled great heights, below the Sperry Glacier dropped sharply into the dense forest of the Pacific Slope. There were bears there. We saw seven at one time the next day, six black and one silver tip, on the very trail he had covered.

But he got the picture.

Once over the crest of the Gunsight, there was a change in the air. It blew about us, warm with the heat it had gathered in the South Pacific. Such animal life as the altitude permitted was out, basking in the sun. There were still snow-fields in the shadows, but they were not so numerous. The rocks threw back the sun-rays on to our burned faces. The trail dipped, climbed, dipped again. Here on a ledge was a cry, "Pack-train coming," and we halted to let pass by a train of men on horseback and of laden little burros, tidy and strong.

Climbing again, the trail was lost in the shale, and arrows painted on the rocks gave us the direction. Two lakes lay together below. One appeared from our elevation rather higher than the other. Rather higher! The rock wall that separated them was fourteen hundred feet high, and vertical.

As we began the last descent, the party grew silent. It was the last leg of the journey. A day or so more and we should be scattered over the continent on whose spine we were so incontinently tramping. Back to civilization, to porcelain bathtubs and course dinners and facial massage, to stays and skirts, to roofs and servants and the vast impedimenta of living.

Sperry Chalet and luncheon. No more the ham and coffee over a wood fire, the cutting of much bread on a flat stone. Here were tables, chairs, and linen. Alas, there was a waitress who crumbed the table and brought in dessert.

Back, indeed, with a vengeance. But only to the ways of civilization itself. All afternoon we went on, descending always, through the outriders of the forest to the forest itself. Dusk came, dusk in the woods, with strange soft paddings of unseen feet, with a gray light half-religious, half-faëry, that only those who penetrate to the hearts of great forests can know.

"It makes me think of death," some one said in a low tone. "Just a great shadow, no color. Nothing real. And silence, and infinite distance."

Then Lake Macdonald. We burst out of the forest on a run. The horses had known, by the queer instinct of horses, that just ahead would be oats and a corral and grass for the eating. They broke into a canter. The various things we had hung to ourselves during the long, slow progress over the mountain rattled and banged. We hung on in a kind of mad exultation. We had done it. We had crossed the Continental Divide, the Lewis Overthrust, whatever geographers choose to call it.

The trail led past a corral, past a vegetable garden such as our Eastern eyes had seldom seen. Under trees, around a corner at a gallop. Then the Glacier Hotel at Lake Macdonald, generally known as "Lewis's."

Soft winds from the Pacific blew across Lake Macdonald and warmed us. Great strawberries were ripening in the garden. Our horses got oats, all they could eat. In a pool in front of the hotel lazy trout drifted about.

There was good food. Again there were people dressed in civilized raiment, people who looked at us and our shabby riding-clothes with a disdain not unmixed with awe. There was fox-trotting and one-stepping, in riding-boots, with an orchestra. And that night at Lewis's they gave Howard Eaton a potlatch.

A potlatch is an Indian party. An Indian's idea of a party is to give away everything he possesses and then start all over again. That is one reason why our Indians are so poor to-day. We sat in a great lobby hung with Indian trophies and bearskins, sat in a circle with Howard Eaton in the center. There were a few speeches and some anecdotes. Then the potlatch went on.

There were hot fried trout, sandwiches, and chips of dried meat—buffalo and deer, I believe. There was beer. After that came the gifts. Everybody got something. Howard Eaton received a waistcoat made of spotted hide, and the women got necklaces of Indian beads. It was extraordinary, hospitable, lavish, and—Western. To have a party and receive gifts is one thing, but to have a party so you can give away things is another.

Seven

The Black Marks

THE VISIT TO THE EXECUTIVE DEPARTMENT OF THE PARK WAS disappointing. I found the superintendent's office in a two-room frame shack; the Government warehouse an old barn: five miles from a railroad, too. That's management for you! Why, O gentlemen at Washington who arrange these things, why not at Belton, on the railroad, five miles away? The park extends to Belton.

Inadequate appropriations, the necessity for putting the entire heavy machinery of the Government in motion for the long-distance control of the park, poor automobile roads, and insufficient rangers—these are the black marks against us in Glacier Park. On every hand the enthusiasm of a most efficient superintendent must contend with these things. That marvels of trail-making and road-building in this vast domain have been done with so little money and encouragement is due, primarily, to the faith the men closely connected with the park have had in its future.

Doubtless all these things will remedy themselves in time. But they make the immediate problems of the park difficult to cope with. The chief ranger must live where he can. No building erected by the superintendent must cost over one thousand dollars. It is not easy in that country of cheap wood and dear labor to build a house for one thousand dollars.

And there is always the difficulty of long-distance supervision. In 1914 the former Superintendent of National Parks, Mr. Daniels, spent a week in Glacier Park. Last year he was at the entrance, Glacier Park Station, for a half a day, and not in the park at all.

There are several parks, and it is easy to believe that Mr. Daniels found it difficult to visit them all. But the method must be wrong. It is Washington that must order and pay for each bit of new trail- and road-building. If Washington does not come to the park, the park cannot go to Washington. There is something lacking in efficiency in a system which depends on across-the-continent supervision.

This year I hope the Superintendent of National Parks will go out to Glacier Park, not by automobile, but on a horse, and ride over his great domain. Then I hope he will go back to Washington and arrange for enough rangers to make the park safe and to save its timber from forest fires. Yellowstone Park has soldiers. It is not soldiers, but woodsmen, trail-riders, rangers, that are needed. Canada, in this same country, has her Northwest Mounted Police.

They want real men out there. But the mountains take care of that. The weaklings don't stick. From just north of Glacier Park went a band of twenty-five cavalrymen that I met last year in Flanders. They were rangers: mountain riders. For weeks during the German invasion they rode on skirmish duty between the advancing Germans and the retiring armies. They became famous. Where there were reckless courage and fine horsemanship needed, those men were sent.

If we ever have a war, we shall draw hard on the West for cavalry. Our national parks should be able to send out trained skirmishers. Under present conditions Glacier Park could furnish about a dozen.

And, now that we are criticizing,—every one may criticize the Government: it is the English blood in us,—why is it that, with the most poetic nomenclature in the world,—the Indian,—one by one the historic names of peaks, lakes, and rivers of Glacier Park are being replaced by the names of obscure Government officials, professors in small universities, unimportant people who go out there to the West and memorialize themselves on Government maps? Each year sees some new absurdity. What names in the world are more beautiful than Going-to-the-Sun and Rising-Wolf? Here are Almost-a-Dog Mountain, Two-Medicine Lake, Red Eagle—a few that have survived.

Every peak, every butte, every river and lake of this country has been named by the Indians. The names are beautiful and romantic. To preserve them in a Government reservation is almost the only way of preserving them at all. What has happened? Look over the map of Glacier Park. The Indian names have been done away with. Majestic peaks, towering buttes are being given names like this: Haystack Butte, Trapper Peak, Huckleberry Mountain, the Guard House, the Garden Wall. One of the most wonderful things in the Rocky Mountains is this Garden Wall. I wish I knew what the Indians called it. Then there are Iceberg Lake, Florence Falls, Twin

Lakes, Gunsight Mountain, Split Mountain, Surprise Pass, Peril Peak,—that last was a dandy! Alliterative!—Church Butte, Statuary Mountain, Buttercup Park. Can you imagine the inspiration of the man who found some flowery meadow between granite crags and took away from it its Indian name and called it Buttercup Park?

The Blackfeet are the aristocrats among American Indians. They were the buffalo hunters, and this great region was once theirs. To the mountains and lakes of what is now Glacier Park, they attached their legends, which are their literature.

The white man came, and not content with eliminating the Indians, he went further and wiped out their history. Any Government official, if he so desires, any white man seeking perpetuation on the map of his country, may fasten his name to a mountain and go down in the school geographies. It has been done again and again. It is being done now. And the lover of the old names stands helpless and aghast.

Is there no way to stop this vandalism? Year after year goes by, and just as the people connected with the park are beginning to learn new names for the peaks, they are again rechristened. There must be seven Goat Mountains. Here and there is a peak, like Reynolds Peak or Grinnell Mountain, and some others, properly named for men intimately associated with the region. But Reynolds's Indian name was Death-on-the-Trail. When you have seen the mountain you can well believe that Death-on-the-Trail would fit it well.

There are many others. Take an old peak that the Indians have known as Old-Man-of-the-Winds or Red-Top Plume and call it Mount Thompson or Mount Morgan or

Mount Pinchot or Mount Oberlin—for Oberlin College, presumably—or Mount Pollack—after the Wheeling stogie, I suppose!

There is hardly a name in the telephone directory that is not fastened to some wonderful peak in this garden spot of ours. Not very long ago I got a letter—a pathetic letter. It said that a college professor from an Eastern college had been out there this summer and insisted that one of the peaks be named for him and one for his daughter. It was done.

Here, then, the Government has done a splendid thing and done it none too well. It has preserved for the people of the United States and for all the world a scenic spot so beautiful and so impressive that I have not even attempted to describe it. It is not possible. But it has failed to open up the park properly. It has been niggardly in appropriation. It has allowed its geographers to take away the original Indian names of this home of the Blackfeet and so destroy the last trace of a vanishing race.

Were it not for the Great Northern Railway, travel through Glacier Park would be practically impossible. Probably the Great Northern was not entirely altruistic, and yet I believe that Mr. Louis Warren Hill, known always as "Louie" Hill, has had an ideal and followed it—followed it with an enthusiasm that is contagious. And with an inspiring faith.

The Great Northern has built huge hotels in three places and at a dozen other locations has built groups of log houses, Swiss fashion, so that it is possible to follow the trails by day and to be comfortably housed and fed each night.

These hotels, built by the Great Northern, are now owned and controlled by the Glacier Park Hotel Company.

At the entrance to the park is the Glacier Park Hotel that cost half a million dollars and is almost as large as the National Capitol at Washington. Like all the hotels and chalets in the park, it is constructed largely of the huge trunks of the trees of the Northwest. The Indians call the Glacier Park Hotel the "Great Log Lodge." There is everything from a store to a swimming-pool.

Fifty miles away in the very heart of the park there is the new Many Glaciers Hotel. It also cost a half-million dollars. There is an automobile road leading to Many Glaciers.

The chalet system, also built by the Great Northern, has done more than anything else to make the park possible for tourists. Automobile roads and trails alike touch the chalets, and, although I am firm in my conviction that it is impossible to see the park properly from an automobile, I realize that there are many who will not take the more arduous and sportsmanly method. For them, then, a short trip of twelve or fifteen miles each day takes them from chalet to chalet. There are chalets at Two-Medicine Lake, at Cutbank Canyon, at Going-to-the-Sun, at St. Mary's Lake, at Gunsight Pass, at the Sperry Glacier, at Granite Park, and at Belton.

There are inclusive and very moderate rates for various tours to take up a certain number of days. A saddle-horse costs two dollars a day; a pack-horse two dollars a day; a guide, who will furnish his own horse and board himself, five dollars a day.

There are rates from chalet to chalet—including a night's lodging in comfortable beds, morning breakfast, evening dinner, and a carefully packed luncheon—that are astonishingly cheap. For those who wish to go even more simply, there are the tepee camps. There are three of these, at St. Mary's, Going-to-the-Sun, and Many Glaciers. They comprise a number of Indian tepees grouped about a central cabin which includes a kitchen provided with a range and cooking utensils. The tepees themselves are wooden-floored and each is equipped with two single cot beds and bedding.

At all of the tepee camps the charge for lodging is fifty cents per bed per night; the use of the range and cooking utensils is free. At the chalets near by, hikers may purchase food at very reasonable prices.

It is, you see, possible to go through Glacier Park without Howard Eaton. It is even safe, and, to those who have never known Howard, highly satisfactory. But there will be something missing—that curious thing called personality, which could take forty-two entirely different, blasé, feeble-muscled, uncertain, and effete Easterners and mould them in a few days into a homogeneous whole: that took excursionists and made them philosophers and sportsmen.

He was hunting in Arizona later on. The party ate venison, duck, and mountain lion—which tastes like veal.

"We have had several fights with grizzlies," he wrote. "They are so strong that they have whipped the hounds and carved them up some in each fight. Country pretty rough and considerable fallen timber, which delays us. I was kicked the other day by a horse when almost up to a bear. The boys thought I had a broken leg or two, so they let the bear escape."

He was sending a rider off to the nearest post-office and wondering what was doing in the war.

"Has Port Arthur fallen yet?" he inquired whimsically.

A hunter who puts the greenest tenderfoot at ease and teaches him without apparently teaching at all; a host whose first thought is always for his guests; a calm-faced man with twinkling blue eyes, who is proud of his "boys" and his friends all over the world—that is Howard Eaton as nearly as he can be put on paper.

Wherever he is when he reads this, hunting in Arizona or the Jackson Hole country, or snowed in at the ranch at Wolf, I hope he will forgive me for putting him into print, in memory of those days when the entire forty-two of us followed him, like the tail of a kite, across the Great Divide.

EIGHT

Bears

IT WAS THE NEXT DAY THAT I MADE MY FIRST CLOSE acquaintance with bears. There are many bears in Glacier Park. Firearms are forbidden, of course, and the rangers kill them only in case of trouble. Naturally, so protected, they are increasing rapidly. They find good forage where horses would starve. Mr. Ralston, the park supervisor, saw a she bear with three cubs last spring. There are no tame bears, as in the Yellowstone.

There are plenty of animals. Some fifty moose graze along the Flathead. Beavers have colonies in many of the valleys and industriously build dams that deepen the fords. I remember one place along the Cutbank Trail where the first horses found themselves above the belly in water and confronting a perpendicular bank up which one or two scrambled as best they could. The rest turned and, riding in the stream for a half-mile détour, made the trail again. That was the work of beavers.

There are coyotes a-plenty. Because they kill the deer and elk, the rangers poison them in the winter with strychnine. A few mountain lions remain. As one can make a whole night hideous, a few are sufficient.

There is something particularly interesting about a bear. Perhaps it is because he can climb a tree. In other words, ordinary subterfuges do not go with him. Reports vary—he is a fighter; he is a craven; the fact being, of course, that he is, like all wild animals and most humans, a bit of each.

The trip was over, and I had seen but one bear. At Lewis's that last Sunday I voiced my disappointment. Soon after I received word quietly that Frank Higgins, guide and companion on many hunting trips to Stewart Edward White and other hunters, had offered to show me some bears.

He had horses saddled under a tree when I went back, and two men, one of them a Chicago newspaper artist, were with him. We mounted and rode up the trail back of the hotel.

I was dubious. For days I had tried to see bears and failed, and now to have them offered with certainty by Mr. Higgins made me skeptical. I had an idea that under his tall impassiveness he was having a little fun at my expense. He was not. We went out into the forest, to where the hotel dumps its garbage. That was rather a blow, at first. And there were no bears. Only a great silence and a considerable stench.

We got off our horses, tied them, and sat down on a log. Almost immediately there was a distant crackling of branches.

"One coming now," said Frank Higgins. "Just sit quiet."

That first bear, however, was nervous. He circled around us. I set my camera for one hundred feet, and waited. But the creature, a big black, was shy. He refused to come out. Mr. Higgins went after him. He snarled. I looked after Mr. Higgins with a new respect, and the Chicago newspaper man said he was perfectly satisfied with the bear where he was, and that enough was enough.

The bear suddenly took to a tree, climbing like a cat. He looked about the size of a grand piano. Urged by Mr. Higgins, we approached the tree. Finally we stood directly beneath. He growled—the bear, of course, not Frank Higgins. But my courage was rising. Wild bear he was, but he was a craven. I moved up the focus of my camera and took his picture. We left him there and went back to the log. All at once there were bears in every direction, six in all. I moved my camera to thirty feet and snapped another. They circled about, heads turned toward us. Now and then they stood up to see us better. We were between them and supper.

The newspaper man offered to sketch me with a "bear" background. And he did. Now and then he would say:—

"Isn't there one behind me?"

"About twenty feet away," I would say.

"Good Lord!" But he went on drawing. I have that picture now. It is very good, but my eyes have the look of a scared rabbit.

Our friend still clung in the tree. The other man had ridden back to the hotel for camera films. Time went on and he did not return. We made would-be facetious remarks about his courage—from our own pinnacle. Almost an hour! The sketch was nearly finished, and twilight was falling. Still he had not come. Then he appeared. He had taken the wrong trail, and had been riding those bear-infested regions alone. He was smiling, but pale. To visit bears in a party is one thing; to ride alone, with fleeting black and brown figures skulking behind fallen timber, is another. Not for a long time, I think, will that gentleman forget the hour or so when he was lost in the forest, with bears

"Thick as autumnal leaves that strew the brooks,
In Vallombrosa."

The poetic quotation is my own idea. What he said was entirely different. As a matter of fact, his own expression was: "Hell, the place is full of them!"

At last, very quietly, Mr. Higgins got up.

"Here's a grizzly," he said. "You might stand near the horses."

We did. The grizzly looked the exact size of a seven-passenger automobile with a limousine top, and he had the same gift of speed. The black bears looked at him and ran. I looked at him and wanted to. The artist put away his sketch, and we strolled toward the horses. They had not objected to the black bears, beyond watching them with careful eyes. But now they pulled and flung about to free themselves. Wherever he goes, a grizzly bear owns his entire surroundings. He carries a patent of ownership.

He could have the woods, for all of me.

The black bears were in full retreat. A hound dog came loping up the trail and caught the scent. In an instant he was after them. Any hope I had ever had of outrunning a bear died then and there. The dog was running without a muffler. One of his frantic yelps changed to a howl as the rearmost bear turned and swatted him. A moment, and the chase was on again.

There is only one thing to do if a bear takes a sudden dis-like to one. It is useless to climb or to run. Go toward it and try kindness. Ask about the children, in a carefully restrained tone. Make the Indian sign that you are a friend. If you have a sandwich about you, proffer it. Then, while the bear is staring at you in amazement, turn and walk quietly away.

It was growing dark. The grizzly, having driven off the black bears, turned his attention to us. We decided that it was almost dinner time, and that we did not care to be late. Anyhow, we had seen enough bears. Enough is enough. We mounted and rode down the trail.

Not all game is as plentiful as bears in Glacier Park or thrives so well. With the cutting-up of the range many of them have lost their winter grazing-grounds. Practically the last of the Rocky Mountain sheep and goats are in Glacier Park. Last winter numbers of these increasingly rare animals were found dead by the rangers. That is another thing the Government will do eventually. It may never see that the Blackfeet Indians have a square deal, but it will feed what is left of the game.

There is little of the old West left. Irrigation, wheat, the cutting-up of the Indian reservations into allotments, the homesteader, all spell the end of the most picturesque period of America's development.

Not for long, then, the cow-puncher in his gorgeous chaps, the pack-train winding its devious way along the trail. The boosting spirit has struck the West. Settlements of one street and thirteen houses, eleven of them saloons, are suddenly becoming cities. The railroads and the automobiles, by obliterating time, have done away with distance. The old West is almost gone. Now is the time to see it—not from a train window; not, if you can help it, from an automobile, but afoot or on horseback, leisurely, thoroughly.

NINE

Down the Flathead Rapids

THE TRIP WAS OVER. I HAD SEEN SUCH THINGS AS I HAD NEVER dreamed of. I had done things which I intended to relate at home. But I had caught no fish to amount to anything. On a Monday night I was to take the train East. On Sunday came great tales of the Flathead River. But I had only one more day. How was it possible?

It was possible. Everything is possible to those Western-ers. I could put on my oldest clothes and fish the Flathead for twenty miles or so the following day under the guidance of one George Locke, celebrated trout-sleuth. Then, rod and fish and all, I could take the Great Northern Eastern Express at a sta-tion and start on my three days' journey home. I did it.

I can still see the faces of the people in that magnificent club car when a woman in riding-clothes, stained and torn, wearing an old sweater and a man's hat, and carrying a camera, a fishing-rod, and a cutthroat trout weighing three and a half pounds, invaded their bored and elegant privacy. The woman was burned to a deep cerise. She summoned the immacu-late porter and held out the trout to him. He was very dubi-ous about taking it. Thereupon the woman put on her most impressive manner and told him how she wished it placed on the ice and how the cook was to fix it and various other details.

It had been a day to live for. The Flathead River does not flow; it runs. It is a series of rapids, incredibly swift, with here and there a quiet pool. Attempts to picture the rapids as we ran them were abortive. We reeled and wallowed, careened and whirled. And always the fisherman-guide was calm, and the gentleman who engineered the party was calm, and I pretended to be calm.

At the foot of each rapids we fished. I was beginning to learn that twist of the wrist that sends out the line in curves, and drops the fly delicately on to the surface of the water.

As I learned, so that he did not close his eyes each time I raised my rod, George Locke told of the Easterner he had taken down the river some time before.

"He wanted a lesson in casting," he said. "And I worked over him pretty hard. I told him all I knew. Then, after I'd told him all I knew, and he'd had all the fun with me he wanted, he just stood up in the bow of the boat and put out ninety feet of line without turning a hair. Cast?

"He could have cast from a spool of thread."

In a boat behind us was a moving-picture man. For weeks he had always been just behind or just ahead. When the time came to leave the West, I missed that moving-picture man. He had come to be a part of the landscape. I can still see him trying to get past us down those rapids, going at lightning speed to gain some promontory where he could set up his weapon and catch our boat in case it upset or did anything else worth recording.

He had two pieces of luck on that trip. I had hooked my first trout and was busy trying to throw it in the boatman's face when it escaped. He caught me at the exact instant when the triumph of my face turned to a purple rage; and later on in the day he had the machine turned on me when I caught two trout on two flies at the same time. Incidentally, I slipped off the stone I was standing on at the same moment. He probably got that, too.

I caught twelve trout in as many minutes from that same rock and furnished the luncheon for the party. I took back loudly everything I had said against the fishing in Glacier Park. I ate more trout than anybody else, as was my privilege. If there were nothing else to it, I would still go back to the Montana Rockies for the fishing in the Flathead River.

At noon we stopped for luncheon. The trout was fried with bacon, and coffee was made. We ate on a little tongue of land around which the river brawled and rushed.

From the time we had left Lake McDermott we had seen no single human being. Mostly the river ran through tall can-yons of its own cutting; always it looked dangerous. Generally, indeed, it was! But never once did the boatman lose control. It reminded me of the story Mark Twain told of the passenger who says to the pilot something like this:—

"I suppose you know where every hidden rock and sunken tree and sandbar is in this river?"

To which the pilot replies: "No, sir-ee. But I know where they ain't."

The train swung on into the summer twilight, past the ruins of old mining-towns, now nothing but names, past brawling streams and great deep woods.

The large trout was cooked and served. It had been worth the effort. There were four of us to eat it—the moving-picture man, the chief ranger of the park, the gentleman from St. Paul who had engineered the fishing-trip, and myself.

At Glacier Park Station my wardrobe, which I had not seen for weeks, was put on the train. "They do you very well," as the English say, in the West. Everything was pressed. Even my shoes had been freshly polished.

A crowd of people had gathered at the station. My supper companions left the train. There were many good-byes. Then the train moved slowly off. I stood on the platform as long as I could and watched the receding lights. Behind the hotel rose the purple-black silhouette of the mountains, touched with faint gold by the lingering finger of the sun.

Stealthy coyotes had taken advantage of the dusk to creep close to the track. A light glimmered from a tent on the Indian reservation. Flat, treeless country, a wagon drawn by tired horses, range cattle that were only shadows.

Then night—and the East.

THE END

About the Author

Mary Roberts Rinehart (August 12, 1876–September 22, 1958) was an American writer who has frequently been called the American Agatha Christie. Wildly popular in the 1910s and 1920s, her mystery novels are still read and referenced in the twenty-first century. She toured the newly minted Glacier National Park with Howard Eaton in 1915, and went on to travel widely throughout the West. Her travelogues helped popularize the national parks and outdoor recreation opportunities and offer a glimpse into an earlier time that is still appealing today.